MW01244367

RESILIENCE

Bend, don't break

KOLLIN L. TAYLOR

Mortified Books
442 Wagon Avenue
Pataskala, OHIO 43062
www.mortifiedbooks.com

Copyright © 2012 Kollin L. Taylor

All rights reserved.

ISBN-13: 978-0-9883296-9-0

Dedication

To Shannon. Thanks for your unconditional love.

Table of Contents

Acknowledgments

My Heavenly Father – I thought that after 260+ poems in two months that my soul was empty. Thanks for teaching me that as long as YOU are in my life, my soul will never be empty. Consequently, YOUR will, will be done and I will continue to write as YOU see fit. Thanks for YOUR countless blessings.

CD –Wherever I go in life, I hope that I never forget everything that you did for me. Thank you for your continued support and for sometimes saying that one word that triggers deep thought that inspires me to write.

Chaplain Miller – Thank you for everything.

Karen Reivich, Ph.D. – Thanks for the many lessons you taught me, and so many others, on being resilient.

Note: Dr. Reivich is the coauthor of the book 'The Resilience Factor'. She has dedicated numerous hours to teaching others, especially members of the military, on how to be resilient.

Special Thanks

My Comrades in Arms – Our duties require a certain degree of toughness. However, sometimes the toughest thing to do is to ask for much needed help. We are formidable, not invincible. Being too tough means we will break under continued pressure. We have to find ways be flexible and strong to handle our duties and what life throws at us.

Introduction

I am not perfect. I fall, and I rise. I make mistakes, and I seek forgiveness. I get hurt, and then I heal. But, I always try to find the silver lining in the clouds of my life; sometimes they find me. I also give thanks every day for everything that I have. Things sometimes take a while to come by, and seemingly, a split second to lose. I won't always win, but it won't stop me from feeling like a winner. I can get badly beaten today, and feel like I will win the rematch the following day. I am not delusional; I am resilient and so are you. If you don't believe me, continue reading as I explore cases of resilience. By the time you reach the end, I hope you'll realize that your capacity to recover from life's challenges is far greater than you probably ever imagined.

You will notice that this book is a testament to my personal resilience. Join me along my journey, as I get pulled back into the darkness and attempt to claw my way out. Continue reading to find out how I did, and what you can do when the light in your life is reduced to a flicker, and there is no fuel in sight.

RESILIENCE

I am Resilient!

I am resilient!
This is something I know,
I'm not about the talk,
I'm about the walk and the show.

Resilience is not about the angst,
Betrayal, or the pain.
Resilience is about the fight,
To drive your life's train.

Resilience is not about quitting,
When you've gotten all you can take.
It's about turning things around,
Even if it takes a lucky break.

Resilience is about,
Making dreams come true.
Even if the only one who believes,
Just happens to be you.

Empty my Soul

I started writing because I wanted to empty my soul.
But now I know that's an impossible goal.
A broken heart created a cleft.
I wanted to purge my system, until there was nothing left.

But that's when I began to see,
I'm never empty because YOU'RE always with me.
So day-by-day, I'll take things in stride,
Walking with YOU, deep inside.
Despite my initial plight,
As long as YOU let me, I'll continue to write.

The Weekend

A baby was born,
A relationship died.
A weekend with sorrow,
And lots of pride.
I just received a call,
About an attempted suicide.

Luckily, things were not as bad as they seemed.
What I just said was real, not something I dreamed.
My words were not inspired by thought,
This is what the weekend brought.

Complete

You lost your legs, an arm and an eye.
Some would have quit, but you try and you try.
When I first saw you I wanted to cry.
Now you inspire me and here's why.

Sports are essentially just a game.
Whether for a weekend warrior, or an athlete of fame.
However, when it comes to you, sports aren't the same.
You give the word 'sport' a more powerful name.

You're not missing anything, you're complete.
I watch in amazement as you compete.
With the bow in your hand, and the arrow in your teeth,
Scoring a bull's-eye was a phenomenal feat.

You practice for hours while drenched in perspiration,
You compete, and serve as a source of inspiration.
An athlete proudly representing your nation,
And to everyone you provide true motivation.

You remind us to never quit,
Whether we stand, crawl, hobble or sit.
You find ways to stay physically and mentally fit.
When I need a picture of resilience – you are it.

Mirage

This is my day to take it easy and be cool.
The highlight of my day is usually hitting the pool.
But this time it was different because of one thought,
I had heartbreaking flashbacks that weren't even sought.

A few minutes at the pool I looked through the screened fence.
What happened next just didn't make sense.
I thought I saw someone who I'd probably date.
But a few seconds later, she looked like someone I should hate.

I can't say who it was because I'm not sure,
It was a quick glance and I didn't see her anymore.
The devil knows this is my day for resilience.
And he ruined it with a peek through the fence.

I tried to swim and play with the ball.
But nothing I did cleared my mind at all.
All this made me slide back down a slippery slope.
But after previous events, I had packed climbing shoes and rope.

A bull can throw me off and I'll get back on without being scared.
Experience has taught me how to come back prepared.
So for a while I'll reminisce,
About the good times and things that I miss.

It's dark now but I hope that by dawn,
All of these thoughts and feelings will be gone.
With everything you know there's nothing to admit.
Life still goes on even after you quit.

So even when someone's not near,
That doesn't mean you won't still care.
Next Sunday, if the weather is clear,
As long as the pool is open, I'll be there.

Delusional

My heart was once broken,
Into tiny pieces by you.
Several people could have stopped it,
By giving me a clue.
And once my heart was broken,
Some could have provided the glue.
But there was no help from them,
And definitely none from you.

But it turned out,
This was something I had to go through.
It was going to be with someone,
It just happened to be with you.

Getting through each day,
Is not always easy to do.
Especially today,
After I saw that mirage of you.

As it turns out,
I have more growing to do.
And I was delusional,
When I thought I was over you.

While I'm still suffering,
And still feeling blue.
I know GOD, family, friends,
And resilience will get me through.

I really thought I was better,
And I had no more tears for you.
But then I saw a guy and a girl,
Who reminded me of when we were two.

All of this time,
Still pining over you.

Despite being shot several times over,
By arrows that went straight through.
I've heard about love,
And now I have a clue.
I really thought I was over,
Feeling anything for you.

Eternal Light

I'm not a doctor,
And I'll probably never be.
But I am a beacon of hope,
And you can rely on me.

I'm also trained to serve others,
As a MRT.
That's a Master Resilience Trainer,
And proud as can be.

Every day I have to look for things,
That improved life for me.
Because even during the darkest nights,
Stars are things I see.
So there is never total darkness,
When it's dark for me.

And then there is something,
That's almost guaranteed to be.
The darkness will give way,
When the sun rises above the sea.

Note: This is based on the following thought that I shared with someone who was going through a tough time: "The stars will still shine during the darkest of nights. But rest assured the sun will rise in the morning."

Familiar Place

I need something to make me feel good,
Because right now, I don't feel like I should.
I was just awakened by a phone call,
After three hours asleep, I'm not rested at all.

I'm still haunted by the pain.
I got some sleep but there was no rest for my brain.
I thought I was over the hurt,
But I find myself back in the dirt.
I'm back in a familiar dark spot.
All I can say is, "Thanks a lot."

It only took a little slip to slide down the slope.
And now I'm hanging on by this rope.
But I'm glad I have a strong grip,
And I'm resilient enough to make the recovery trip.
The climb back up may be hard,
But in my game of life, there's no "I quit" card.

If that girl only knew,
That even as of today she has me feeling blue.
I wonder how she would feel,
If she only knew what I felt was real?
The truth is she doesn't care,
These are my feelings and not for her to share.

I didn't do something to lose control.
Someone pushed me back in this hole.
It was a test and I failed.
So mentally I got jailed.

I'm back in solitary confinement,
For more growth and refinement.

This darkness I have to embrace,
Even though the sun may shine on her face.
Does any of this ever cause her pain?
She may not even remember my name.
Plus there's nothing she can do,
She doesn't need to know, or get a clue.

But I'll get out of here,
Whether it takes a day, or a year.
The darkness is followed by light.
I'll keep on trying and keep my goals in sight.
I've recovered from this once before.
And I only need to do it once more.

House Cleaning

I've said, "Help Me!" while trying to get well.
But those who could help only opened the gates to my hell.
They have to deal with their own pain.
And helping me gives them very little to gain.

Many know what I'm going through.
Yet they treat me like they don't have a clue.
They go for days without answering my email.
And even instant messages fail.

They make my hours seem like days.
They fail to help me through this phase.
I make lots of noise for them to hear,
Yet they treat me like they don't care.

Instead of making things better, they make it worse.
They have the power to help lift this curse.
But there's something that I see,
The power is also in me.

It's time for some house cleaning.
Some friends are about to catch the meaning.
I'll ask one question that requires a yes or no.
If you're not a true friend, you'll have to go.

I'm going to put my train back on the track,
And I'm not going to let anyone hold me back.
I was doing so well,
But you sent me back into this hell.

Patience Equals Resilience

I like when the things I write rhyme, and make sense.
Like the link between patience and resilience.
One thing about problems that affect you and me,
Is that they're all temporary.

There's tension in the atmosphere.
But I learned to cope so it's like there's no tension here.
There was a time when I almost broke.
But even though serious, some things are like a joke.

It's something else when you seemingly just can't win.
And your best efforts go straight to the garbage bin.
Every dark cloud has a bright side.
So I kept doing my best, and topped it off with pride.

Things are better, but still not great,
But they'd be worse if I still carried that hate.
When times are hard, keep moving; don't stop.
Because the crème always rises to the top.
I hope everything I said rang through,
And you see how patience and resilience can work for you.

Resilient Breath

On September 11th, more than 3000 people died,
When our nation was open and they flew inside.
Those acts seemed to mark the nation's death,
But instead it infused a more resilient breath.
We were attacked while we slept,
Soon after, the entire nation wept.

We received the message you sent,
And our answer was to show that we're resilient.
Multiple wars have been fought,
And those responsible were either killed or caught.
The one thing this story will always lack,
Is that nothing can bring those lost lives back.

Smoother Track

This is a story that is often told,
But the story line will still leave you feeling cold.
It's about a young lady, who didn't meet her goal,
Because of a situation where she had very little control.

Unfortunately, what she saved was painfully lost,
But that was only the beginning of the total cost.
This is the part that is bound to displease,
Is when she ended up with a disease.
Luckily it was the type that had a cure,
But it didn't stop her parents from putting her out the door.

And after experiencing the dejection,
She still has problems handling even minor rejection.
Thanks to resilience, she bounced back,
And her life is on a smoother track.

Relief Pitcher

As I got ready to brief,
What happened next was to my disbelief.
What I heard made me break a sweat,
Because the next briefer was not here yet.

I knew my subjects through 'n through,
But for his, I only had a clue.
I just said, "What the heck!"
And I briefed his slide deck.

I tried my best to keep my cool,
And speak without looking like a fool.
On the outside things aren't always how they seem.
But I calmly took one for the team.

Resilience is not all about bouncing back.
Sometimes it means switching from a dead-end track.

Flickering Light

I have a real sour taste in my mouth,
Instead of north, things went south.
The things some people just don't get,
And the things you sometimes regret.

If I could go back in time,
I wouldn't write this rhyme.
Today I thought I was going to get a break.
There was so much at stake.

But things don't always go my way,
Regardless of what I do or say.
Remember my beacon of positivity?
Well, it's running low on energy.

Before things get better, they may get a little worse.
But I'm going to put things in reverse.
Sometimes people can't change your day,
Instead you have to do it your way.

Resilience means even when you're down, you're not out.
Despite the negative forces all about.
Even though I want to throw a fit,
I'm going to fight because I will not quit.

Low Blow

When someone hits you low,
Your best bet is not always a lower blow.
The things you say or do,
Have a tendency to come back at you.

With everything going on, I feel beat down,
For all my efforts, I feel like a clown.
While some people think it's a joke,
My emotional bank is flat broke.

This doggone rollercoaster ride,
Jarred my organs and my pride.
Far and wide, word has spread,
About the poetry flowing from my head.

If they only knew,
That it was from pain that they all grew.
I don't like doing things by force,
But my life needs a new course.

These words are sometimes heaven-sent,
And other times they feel like punishment.
It takes one thing, and this ends,
So one by one, I'm cutting out my so-called friends.

It's easy for me to be a nice guy,
But ungrateful people make me wonder why.
Luckily, and despite feeling blue,
I'm grateful for everything YOU do.

I know in time, I'll bounce back,
But right now, there's baggage in my sack.
I know I'll persevere,
So I need to make the best of what's here.

I've heard about a friend in need,
But I don't see my friend in deed.
My world is almost pitch black,
But I guarantee I'll come back.

Those Who Are Near

It's painfully obvious why I'm here,
Why I'm gloomy and I've lost my cheer.
It's because of those who are near,
Things will be dark as long as they're here.

Maybe they just don't realize,
How their actions look through my eyes.
Or maybe they just don't care.
How I'm affected by what I hear.

People just can't see,
How everything affects me.
There's nowhere to run or hide.
I'll have to fight this rough tide.

While I struggle to battle the sea,
Very few people are here with me.
And if I were to go down,
Most would just watch me drown.

As I look up at the TV,
A lovely sight was revealed to me.
A player came from being down,
To winning the championship crown.

I'll enjoy the bitterness of this state.
The sweetness will come. I'll have to wait.
Turning things around may seem like an impossible feat,
But it's a challenge I'm willing to meet.

Lil' by Lil'

Little by little, bit by bit,
I'm learning to walk versus sit.
My dreams are now about cookies and cake,
But I still have flashbacks about heartbreak.
What we seek, is what we'll find,
All things start in the mind.

The power of thoughts, the power of action,
Getting what we seek can bring satisfaction.
Dreams can be powerful, and some will come true,
The power to heal resides in me and you.

No one can keep me down for too long,
My courage and faith are simply too strong.
I'm not going to lie; I'm not all the way back,
But it's a big powerful heart that I pack.

12th Round

It's the 12th round of a championship fight,
I'm stuck in a corner getting pelted by his left and right.
My eyes are swollen and I'm losing my sight,
I better move soon or a knockout will end this fight.

I was winning, I was in my groove.
For 11 rounds it was stick 'n move.
But sometimes all it takes,
Is one good punch to put on the brakes.

I got too cocky when I had him on his heels,
Now karma is showing me how losing feels.
Even though his punch stings,
I'm fighting till the bell rings.

But for now, I'm going to hug and grab,
Let the ref part us, and reestablish my jab.
I was winning so there's no need to panic,
But I'm going to lose if I remain static.

Being resilient is not always about making a big move,
But you have to shift if you're in the wrong groove.
So until the fight ends I'm keeping up my guard,
I don't need a knockout to win this card.

Because I was careless and made a few slips,
I'm going to have some real fat lips.
And for a while I'm going to be in pain,
But I'm resilient because of how hard I train.

Karaoke

Oh what a sight!
Actually, it was more about the sound.
And how the wrong voice or key,
Can make your ear pound.

I know I sound great,
At least in the shower.
But in this public setting,
I usually cower.

There are some people,
Whose voices are heaven-sent.
Then there are those,
That provide potential embarrassment.

But the best performance,
Of the entire night,
Was a guy who sounded so bad,
It would ruin your hearing and sight.

In the end,
He was a source of inspiration to me.
Because he was resilient,
And that set him free.
He's usually smiling,
And as happy as can be.

It wasn't about what we thought,
He simply didn't care.
He didn't have the voice,
But he had charisma to share.

They say when you look at a dog's tail end,
The view is always crappy.

We could have booed that guy off stage,
And he'd still have been happy.

He was an example,
Of resiliency.
He approached life with zest,
And lots of glee.

Never Forgotten

It's September 11th,
A potentially somber day.
We started it off,
To remember POWs and those who are MIA.

Today we took the time,
And watched the flag as it flied,
But every day,
We remember those who serve with pride.

Whether they're missing,
Were captured, or died.
At our table,
We always have room set aside.

To every end of the earth,
We will roam.
Until our fallen, missing or captured,
Return home.

And to those,
Who are still in enemy hands,
It's behind you,
That a grateful nation stands.

Your Life's Hue

After a week in the dumps,
Way deep in the pit,
I only needed something,
To get me out of it.

I got a little wind,
Put back in my sail,
With a click of the mouse,
To check my email.

Seeing two sample book covers,
Made my dream come true.
It only takes one thing,
To change your life's hue.

Before I was tired,
And dying to sleep.
But my future just got brighter,
And it almost made me weep.

I needed this sunshine,
To brighten this dark hue.
It's amazing to see,
What a simple thing can do.

To my LORD and savior,
I'm resilient because of YOU.
YOU delivered me from the darkness,
Right on cue.

YOU are the master,
At what YOU do.
Thanks for the challenge,
And for getting me through.

Passage of Time

There are still things to this day,
That affect me in a negative way.
There are still people I see,
Who will trigger a bad memory.

But with the passage of time,
It gets easier for me to feel fine.
And getting in a good state of mind,
Is much easier to find.

I'm not always in a state of glee,
But I don't let things get the best of me.
You can't keep me down for long,
I'm a fighter who always comes back strong.

Payback

"It's girls like that who ruin the good men," is what was said.
Those few words have stuck in my heart, and my head.
And while those words are true,
They commit the act, but survival is on you.

Just because someone breaks your heart,
Doesn't mean you should break someone else's apart.
Just because someone knocks you to the ground,
Doesn't mean you should start pushing others around.
Just because someone hurts you real bad,
Doesn't mean you should spend the rest of your life mad.

Sure, the cross is yours to bear,
And it may hurt that they don't care.
Despite anything you're owed,
You have to figure out how to lighten your load.
If you go around harboring hate,
It can ruin your very best trait.

Note

I shared a few of the poems I wrote,
And I was touched by the thank you note.
Emotional pain is something we can hide,
But I shared a message of how to let it outside.
Everything that I went through,
Was to make me better at helping someone like you.
And while you may need to forgive,
I'll help show you how to live.
When darkness blankets your light,
I'll show you how to win the fight.
And when you're alone and filled with fear,
I'll remind you someone is always near.

Rebound

Things have a way of raising its ugly head.
Even though you buried the past, it returns from the dead.
All those lovely lines you were fed,
Turn into something else instead.

But the same way those things sprout from the ground,
Is the same way you can rebound.
When you rise from your darkest day,
Others may have hell to pay.

But hurt and resentment are spread that way.
Do your best to keep your ill feelings at bay.
Because when karma comes your way,
If you caused pain, you will have hell to pay.

Liar, Liar

Her stepdad would sneak into her room at night.
After the first time, she stopped putting up a fight.
She tried to tell her mom, by whispering in her ear.
But she didn't listen, such "lies" she didn't want to hear.
"If you lie like that again, I will kick you out of here!"
Now she's caught between abuse, and another kind of fear.
All because her mother wanted a "man" near.

Her mother kept on living, every day she would pretend,
While for her daughter, the torture didn't end.
The mother got ill and got up late one night,
She thought she was dreaming, because of the terrible sound
and sight.

Her daughter was hurting, but her mother didn't care.
She just locked the door, and left her daughter there.
Before the break of dawn, her daughter ran away.
She found a caring uncle with whom to stay.

That time is now behind her, and she's fully healed,
She wrote a book, and her story was revealed.
She's now a motivational speaker, with another book deal.
But her greatest gift is helping survivors heal.
She's now a woman, with a family of her own.
Every day she experiences a love, like she's never known.

Pier & Sea

When my ship was stuck at the pier,
I don't recall seeing you there.
But now that it's sailing at sea,
You have something to say to me.

Coming to the pier would've been a symbol of care.
But since you weren't there, you can disappear.
It's nice to have a friend, who will pay my bail,
But I need a friend, who will keep me out of jail.
Where were you, when I needed a friend?
If you weren't at the beginning, you won't be in the end.

I know my treatment, may sound a bit harsh,
But you turned my life, into a swampy marsh.
And for you, I once gave my soul,
But it just allowed the devil, to almost take control.

Luckily, many temptations were resisted,
And for quite a while, the bitter taste persisted.
You caused so much pain on more than one instance,
Even though I still love you, I'll do so from a distance.

"It Takes Time"

I took a minute because there was something I wanted to do,
I had to tell CD about how something came through.
CD was busy, so I gave a quick report,
CD smiled. "It takes time, it takes time," was her retort.

I thank her for planting a seed,
And within seconds my brain started to feed.
Her words made me think of why we say 'human race',
And how we like things at a different pace.

I'm mostly patient and can quietly wait,
While someone else may rush out the gate.
There is a time and a place,
To move at a fast or slow pace.

The recent issues with which I've had to deal,
Some are surprised that I've yet to heal.
But most don't know that I'm like the walking dead,
I was killed by things that were done and said.

Imagine being beaten in your bed,
But every night that's where you lay your head.
It's hard to escape that memory,
If you're surrounded by reminders as far as you can see.

Then there are things and people in my presence,
Who are reminders of things that test my resilience.
So it's been a long road to a full recovery,
Because of the things that plague my memory.

It's one thing to return to the scene of a crime,
It's another thing to see reminders all the time.
But thanks to a good friend of mine,
I know I'll recover, but, "It takes time."

No Teeth or Claws

I'm battered and bruised.
Some days I feel emotionally abused.
Someone recently asked if, at this rate,
If there are certain women I'll no longer date.
That wouldn't be right,
At least not in my sight.

Everyone still has an equal opportunity,
When it comes to dating me.
And having discriminating taste,
Is not the same as to discriminate.
The actions of a few,
Shouldn't ruin the chances for those in the queue.

The dating pool is still the same,
I need rank, status, before name.
I'm in a pool filled with fish,
But there's none on my dish.
I'm a bear in a lake while the fish spawn,
But my claws and teeth are gone.

Today I saw a girl smile at a guy,
My first reaction was it's a lie.
That's because of what happened to me,
I don't believe everything I see.
Someone can smile at me that way,
But today would have been a bad day.

I was open to date,
But now the thought makes me irate.
The evil people do,
And then act like they have no clue.

I'm still on the resilient track,
But I have a minor setback.
When someone gets hurt,
They may repeatedly fall back in the dirt.

But in a little while,
I'll have reason to smile.
I'm going to be like a skunk,
And adapt to dealing with the funk.
I'm going to be like a bee,
And use this pain to make honey.

Fats

I'm a snake of the poisonous variety,
I'm docile now, but don't test me.
A diamondback is something you don't want to battle.
Especially if warned by the fangs or rattle.

I'm a snake you can call me Fats.
I have a hood like a bodybuilder's "lats".
I eat other snakes while they eat rats.
But I don't eat dogs or cats.

Around my neck is a ring,
I'm the cobra they call "The King".
You don't want me in a fight.
I don't make noises, I just bite.

There was a time when I was filled with pride,
And I spread my hood real wide.
I had a target in striking distance,
But it got away in that instance.
I couldn't believe that I missed,
And that it never got kissed.

I had a friend named Copperhead.
A car ran over him and the driver thought he was dead.
What the diver found out is that snakes are resilient instead.
Even if you have a gun and you fill us with lead.

Even with our bodies crushed and no signs of life,
We can still bite with fangs that are sharper than a knife.
We're one of nature's ultimate predators, but truth be told,
We're tough, but we hate when it's cold.

Heat 'n Pressure

Heat and pressure can crush blocks.
Heat and pressure also separates diamonds from regular rocks.
There are things that heat and pressure breaks,
And there are things that heat and pressure makes.
Stress can make you feel low,
Stress can also help you grow.
There are a lot of challenges that life will give.
But we choose how we'll continue to live.

Frame-by-Frame

I may look like I'm built like a rock,
But right now, I feel like a sock.
Our mind is like a camera capturing our lives frame-by-frame,
We live with memories that are wild and tame.

For some people, things are easy to forget,
So they move on without regret.
But for some, things aren't the same,
A photographic memory can play back every frame.

The first person I met who was this way,
Was a stunning Iraqi named May.
But here's someone with the same thing too,
She's a celebrity named Mary Lou.

It's a kind of gift that takes special strength,
Because it can make it harder to be resilient.
While most may strive to forgive and forget,
They can recall their every regret.
Their blessing may seem like a curse,
And send healing back in reverse.
We can say memories fade over time,
Not their memories, just yours and mine.

There's someone else I won't mention by name,
But her gift is also the same.
Honesty is the best policy and this is why,
To these ladies, you don't want to lie.

Lonely Screw

For about two years,
A screw was in my wall.
I had absolutely no plans for it,
No plans at all.

That was until CD,
Saw that I wasn't doing the same.
So she got a gift for me,
It was a picture in a frame.

It was a picture,
I'll love seeing for a while.
I'll remember her thoughtfulness,
And it will make me smile.

I took it to my room,
After thanking her a lot.
And that lonely screw,
Marked the perfect spot.

You've gotten to know me,
Much better by now.
Can you guess,
How I'll tie this to resiliency somehow?

Just imagine,
You're alone in a tight spot.
You try to help yourself,
By giving everything you've got.
You'll eventually get through it,
Or maybe someone will give you a shot.

What some may see,
As a simple picture frame.
For me is a reminder,
That resilient is my middle name.

And that friends like CD,
Will get me through my pain.
When times are hard,
It's the good ones who remain.

Ace of Spades

In a deck of cards,
I'm the ace and the spade.
I have a pointy tip,
From the mess you made.
I'm bitter,
From the games you played.
I'm salty,
Because of memories that won't fade.
I'm charcoal black,
From a life without shade.

My favorite county,
Is Miami-Dade.
One of the sexiest women I know,
We called T-Wade.

Gentlemanly ways,
I've still displayed.
The things I keep,
Would get others dismayed.

If I was warned,
I would've still disobeyed.
To get through this,
To GOD I prayed.
And thanked HIM,
For the friends who stayed.
And for blessing me,
Despite the mistakes I made.
And,
Despite anything I may lack,
For strengthening me,
So I always bounce back.

Challenging Feat

I'm glad I'm not easy to confuse.
But I see a confusing trend in the news.
I see beautiful women go through misery,
By falling for men with a bad history.

These women look like a dream,
But they get kicked off the men's team.
They see what the men did before,
But they still enter that door.
I guess they think they have what it takes,
Until their own heart breaks.

Did they fall for those men's charms,
And think they wouldn't cause them harm?
If they have a bad history,
First, you may want to solve the mystery.

Did they love and get hurt before?
So they fear getting hurt once more.
That's a problem with which they must deal,
Or you're the one who'll need to heal.
If they have a fear of commitment,
It's probably going to end with resentment.
If it's a challenge you seek,
Be careful with this kind of feat.

To find out if you're resilient,
You basically have to get bent.
And if there are no breaks,
You know you have what it takes.

But sometimes your very best bet,
Is to avoid things you may regret.
Heartbreak can cause a horrible scene,
And you'll need more than a quart of cookies 'n cream.

Embrace the Pain

As I woke up in my room,
My first sight brought some gloom.
I saw a good friend of mine,
With her daily Valentine.

It was a lovely photo shoot,
Together they looked real cute.
I was happy that she found another,
But it reminded me of being a single brother.

Last night, I walked home with me, myself, & I,
And I really wondered why,
I was feeling so jaded,
And all women were hated.
It was an emotion I had not recently felt,
But that's a card I was dealt.

I sweated and soaked my shirt,
From the heat and the hurt.
For as long as I can remember,
My lowest points related to the other gender.

That doesn't mean I am free of blame,
But my life is not the same.
Now on the weekends,
I'm the only single one among my friends.

But just how the story goes,
How it will end, no one knows.
Here's something for you to do,
Make the best of what life hands you.
I will too, in turn,
As soon as I recover from this burn.

Even though I feel disdain,
I'm learning to embrace the pain.
But on a day like today,
My smile ran away.
I just want to say, "I don't mean to be rude,
Just leave me alone, I'm not in the mood."
But the thing about isolation,
It's not the best insulation.
It causes a worse reaction,
Than human interaction.

Reverberate

I don't like the way I'm filled with hate.
As sights and sounds reverberate.
It's harder to hit pause,
When you don't have a cure, but you're haunted by the cause.

I really have to take time to pray,
That no one rubs me the wrong way.
I know this is a temporary rough patch,
And that the darkness is secured by a latch.

I know what they mean by holding on to a thin rope.
Especially on such a slippery slope.
I see why some people use dope,
But that's never the best way to cope.

In the middle of distress,
You may need others as a source of happiness.
Some like to set an independent tone,
But some things you shouldn't do alone.

It's because I'm in the middle of the stink,
Why to dark depths I can sink.
But this is how I have to feel,
For my words to be real.

It's hard to share my soul,
If I'm still in full control.
If I don't feel like I'm about to fall,
I won't be genuine at all.

The pain has to reverberate,
For you to feel the heartbreak.
And I really have to sink,
For you to smell the stink.

A Spark

In a place so small it's amazing to me.
How much I gather from the little things I see.
Causing a fire only takes a spark.
One small thing can put you in the dark.
If given a choice to sink or swim.
I choose the latter; I'm a survivor, not a victim.

I was inspired by a bulletin board,
By a survivor of a crime while she oared.
It definitely was not her fault,
But it never is for the survivors of an assault.

Despite things that were beyond her control,
She recovered and completed her goal.
Her goal was funds collection,
Instead she became an inspiration.

First Request

A man and his friend were adrift at sea,
He was rescued shortly after month three.
This may sound like a joke,
But his first request was for a smoke.

Eating fish and drinking rainwater kept him alive,
Unfortunately his friend didn't survive.
But I must confide,
I thought his addiction would have also died.

Regardless of his perceived weakness,
One thing I won't dismiss,
Is how he inspired me,
With his resiliency.

Stronger Than Steel

There are things that in time,
GOD will reveal.
And after all of your suffering,
You will heal.

I know right now,
You hate the raw deal,
I've had my share,
And can imagine how you feel.

Sometimes you wonder,
If it's a dream or if it's real.
You're out in the cold,
Like a fruit without its peel.
You're stuck in darkness,
And trapped by a seal.
And fighting to continue,
May lose its appeal.
I can empathize,
With how you may feel.

But the suffering,
Can make you grow stronger than steel.
I'm here for you,
Regardless of how you feel.
That's how you know,
When a friendship is real.

Silver Lining

Every time I've seen you,
You've always had a glow.
But something is different,
I wonder what makes it so.

I know it has been
A very rough year,
You have seen more sadness,
Than you have cheer.
But I know that can happen,
Especially over here.
I admire the way you fought to survive,
Throughout the last year.

With everything you've been through,
I barely have a clue.
But I've seen resilience,
In everything you do.

Now that the clouds,
And storm is going by.
I'm glad that you shared your glow,
And the reasons why.

It's actually sad,
That you have to go.
But it's good to hear,
That love and a baby are the reasons why you glow.

Note: This is based on someone who has lost a lot, struggled, endured, and will come out a stronger person (even though she is more than strong enough right now). Best wishes.

Finally, A Good Day!

For the first in a long time I'm proud to say,
For so many reasons, today was a great day!
It all started when I went to sleep,
And a virtual hug was mine to keep.

And even though I woke up at three,
I wrote two poems that uplifted me.
Then I went back to bed with a smiley face,
With images from my happy place.

Today something happened that made me smile.
I was told something I had not heard in a while.
Those ladies helped to make my day,
Even more than my words can say.
The best thing about the feel,
Is that I knew their words were real.

And I can't forget to mention,
The Chaplain wants to use a poem for suicide prevention.
I also received a special request,
And for that poem I'll do my best.

Everything didn't go my way,
But I didn't let anything ruin my day.
Now when I say, "I can feel it right there!"
It's because I know that victory is near.

Tina Berry

Let me take you back to 1996,
He taught us aerobics and he loved those kicks.
It was no secret so let me say,
We all thought he was gay.

Like a berry he was very sweet,
One of the nicest guys you'll ever meet.
Here's a secret that I'll share,
He could have been open because we didn't care.
He was a Soldier in our ranks all uniformed,
We judged only based on how he performed.

When Tina came out it was no surprise,
She's still a beautiful woman in my eyes.
I'm glad that she no longer has to pretend,
By going on dates in search of a "boyfriend".
She looks so much better that she's free,
To be with her gorgeous girl named Bre.

Things have changed in military life,
Now it really doesn't matter who's your husband or wife.
I want everyone to be free and happy,
How you serve is what matters to me.
I don't care if you're gay or straight,
But I care if you show up late.
I don't care who you date,
If you're happy, that is great!

I'm glad people don't have to live in a shell,
And we no longer have Don't Ask Don't Tell.
Here's one more thing I will state,
Coming out still takes a leap of faith.
I'm sure there're people, who still hide,
Their bisexual, gay, lesbian, and transgender pride.

Before a few people throw up what they ate,
And start thinking this is why we didn't date.
Even though for us it's too late,
I believe in equal opportunity, but I'm still straight.

There're things in life with which we don't agree,
But we can coexist and still be free.
Even in today's day and age,
Interracial dating still causes rage.
Here's the last thing that I'll say,
Do something that makes you happy today.

Is This A Dream?

How far have we come? Let me check.
It's rare to find a rope around a person's neck.
There no longer is a dividing line,
When I go out to dine.
I still admire the courage of Rosa Parks,
And how her defiance caused sparks.

Life is much better I suppose,
No dog bites or getting doused with a fire hose.
Being a janitor was as far as I could go,
Now, I can be the CEO.

Once, I could only run for the team,
Now being a quarterback is a possible dream.
Once, I could only work in the prison's garden,
But now, I'm the prison's warden.

Once, I could only work on military tanks,
Now, I can lead the ranks.
Once, I wasn't really a resident,
Now, I can be the President.

But here's something among the last frontier,
And I'm going to take you there.
For some it may make you irate,
What do you think about people on an interracial date?!

Dr. King spoke about the Promised Land.
Is it buried under layers of sand?
The Promised Land is where you want to be,
It's when the world is color fair, because it will never be color free.

Note: I was asked to write a poem for a function to commemorate Black History Month 2013.

Mental Hustle

Being resilient is an incredible feat,
I marvel at the odds I've seen people beat.
Despite perceived disabilities, I've seen people compete,
And despite strengths, others don't feel complete.

Sometimes people fail,
Because they are trapped in a mental jail.
Sometimes they try to cope with a drug,
Because they stay buried under a rug.

Resilience is a feat of strength that requires no muscle,
To beat the darkness just requires mental hustle.
You have to see those traps and steer clear,
And when you go deep, don some SCUBA gear.

You have to recognize the trend,
That pushes you towards the deep end.
And before you go off the cliff or around the bend,
It helps to have a caring friend.

Chance Encounter

I couldn't believe he was surprised.
All this time and he hadn't realized.
He thought I sounded jaded,
But he never realized how much I had faded.
This time I was wearing a shirt,
My uniform couldn't hide the effects of my hurt.

"Man, what happened? You used to be huge!" he said.
This is what happens after being left for dead.
All this time trying to act with class,
Now he saw my wasted muscle mass.
It doesn't matter what he chooses to say,
He knows how I got this way.

All this time I didn't live, I was only alive,
And to make it through each day I had to strive.
He usually saw me at work and my efforts to persevere.
And now he knows the damage is real severe.
The one thing he may not know,
Is I view the space in my clothes as room to grow.

Paparazzi

I actually feel sorry for Princess Kate,
It also makes me feel irate.
It still fills me with rage,
Even in today's day and age.

Sure she knows she's under scrutiny,
She's always in magazines and on TV.
When she thought she had privacy,
It was ruined by the paparazzi.
What was for her husband's eyes to behold,
Now the whole world has been told.

It's not like she sent a drunken text,
And then posted photos on Twitter next.
She and her husband were on vacation,
But there's no such thing for the future leaders of a nation.

She's on tour as a dignitary,
And despite the release of the imagery,
She has held her head up high,
While on the inside she probably wants to cry.

I like how she carries herself with grace,
And how she puts on a very brave face.
She finds a reason to smile,
Despite the images that will haunt her for a while.

While people tend to have curiosity,
Those are images I don't care to see.
I'm going to respect the man's wife,
And boycott those images for the rest of my life.

Despite the feelings she may have to hide,
I like how her husband stands by her side.
When the going gets really rough,
Companionship helps you hang tough.

Sealed with a Kiss

I woke in the night with a feeling of bliss,
Mentally holding someone new and it was sealed with a kiss.
Between us there was no light,
As we snuggled throughout the night.

Many would say, "Man, it's about time,
It sounds like you may have written your last sad rhyme.
Your deep stories we'll certainly miss.
But to get over someone, find someone else to kiss."

While that is solid advice,
This story won't be that nice.
From my bed, I was kicked to the floor.
I actually felt ruined like others said before.

My thoughts were lost on a lady, who was so cute,
Then you know who came and gave me the boot.
I'm haunted by memories of treating her like a miss,
She loved them, while I got the dis...

I felt like the dogs got the prize,
And the gentleman got a rude surprise.
I remember that comment about what girls like her do,
They take apart men, like a wrecking crew.
Then those men who would have stayed,
Turn around and make women feel played.

But I'm stubborn, and I know that I have to choose,
I won't be ruined, because I refuse.
Sometimes I feel like that was her goal,
To come into my life and destroy my soul.

I'm here to tell you she didn't succeed.
I'm scarred, but time is mostly what I need.
Sure it would help if I found someone new,
So I could tell my ghost adieu.

In the meantime, I'll try to make myself whole,
My recovery is my number one goal.
You may have noticed, I no longer call her name,
The way she turned out is a source of shame.
To this day, she's had nothing to say,
And is comfortable treating me this way.
There's no more venom for me to spew,
May GOD have mercy on you.

Works of Art

Sometimes, it's with watery eyes,
That you find out it's the devil in disguise.
He'll package a gift just for you,
And make it seem all so true.
And when you open what you received,
You later find out, you were deceived.

But that's not where the journey ends,
Let's go through the twist and bends.
It does not end with the initial reception,
Being burned can ruin your perception.

Remember the saying about once bitten twice shy...?
This is an example of why.
Even with common sense, or if you're book smart,
What's fake and real may look like works of art.
The devil will win if you start to feel,
Like everything's fake and nothing is real.

It's hard after being hurt to the core,
But you only lose if you won't try once more.
In time, where you once were deceived,
You'll rejoice for the gift you received.

Validated & Vindicated

I know what I said.
I have no more venom to spew.
This is only a recollection,
Of someone else's point of view.

A friend recently shared some news,
That I gave a warm reception.
It was about an encounter,
And the lasting perception.

All this time in darkness,
And feeling hurt.
According to the feedback,
It was something she was not worth.

I have to admit,
That was my worst fear.
That after everything I'd been through,
People would say she didn't deserve my care.

I like to treat people well,
And never put them down,
But according to the feedback,
I should've flushed her with the brown.

I was told about how she carried herself,
Which confirmed another fear.
What she did to me,
She probably doesn't care.
And it wouldn't be a surprise,
If on that very day,
She was on the prowl,
To find another prey.

My friend said someone did me a favor,
By removing her from my sphere.

And that she looked selfish,
With absolutely nothing to share.

I didn't need to hear this again,
I don't need any more proof.
Based on my friend's observation,
That girl was definitely aloof.

My friend's internal feeling,
Of "Righteous Anger" was almost shared.
There was almost an exchange,
Because of how much my friend cared.

Those who know me,
And know I wasn't doing well,
I have to hold some back,
From giving her a taste of hell.

Then I was told,
That love is truly blind.
Because there're better women,
Out there for me to find.

That's why our friends and family,
Get introduced to our dates.
So they can assess,
How the person rates.

I can no longer defend her,
For everything she did.
And in due time,
She will vanish from my grid.

Those who know her,
Questioned what I saw.
And say she'll learn a painful lesson,
When karma grabs her with its claw.

Most people I know,
Have truly put her down.

But making her look bad,
Is not what gets rid of my frown.

She had choices,
And probably never regretted those she made.
But how I impacted other people's lives,
Is how I get paid.
As time goes by,
Feelings and memories fade.
People tell me,
She'll be sorry for the decision she made.

And despite how she treated me,
Others would like me in their life.
They would love me as a husband,
And happy to be my wife.

So for a brief time,
My former love and my friend shared space.
But my friend told me,
That I'm in a better place.

My friend's vision,
Is even better than sight.
Whatever my friend saw,
I have to believe it's right.

Maybe one day I will know,
Maybe one day I will see.
But I'm glad I pulled through,
Thanks to support and resiliency.

Despite everything,
Here's what really gives me pause.
I hate quitting on someone,
As if they were a lost cause.
I realize that some things,
Are really not my fight.
Especially if their conscience is clear,
And they sleep well at night.

But this is the price I pay,
For the world that I see.
This life that I live,
Is far bigger than me.

A Friend From Near & Far

I feel like pepper spray is burning my face.
Events today have darkened my space.
This darkness in my presence,
Is weighing heavily on my resilience.

But even though I felt that way,
I had a friend who made my day.
When bad things are on your mind,
There's only one good thing you need to find.
For me it's something that was said,
That played back in my head.
The things a friend can say,
Has the power to make your day.
Bad memories started taking me there,
But my friend's words brought me cheer.
It turned my day around,
Until happiness was found.

One day I may see,
About what my friend said to me.
It doesn't have to be true,
As long as it feels good to you.
That's not to say one should lie,
And preserving your credibility is why.
But whatever is said,
Must make sense and feel good in their head.
So even though I was alone,
My friend still threw me a bone.

Hurts so Good

Love is beautiful; it's all good.
There is no hurt if you love like you should.
Except for when you love with every fiber of your being,
And stars and butterflies are things you are seeing.
When you can say that person is mine,
And they are your daily Valentine.

But that's a different kind of pain,
It drives you wild, not insane.
That's when you love like you should,
And it hurts, but it hurts real good.

But for me to reach this point,
I had to escape from a real bad joint.
It was filled with heartbreak,
From a love that was actually fake.
But I bounced back with zeal,
And now I feel a love that's real.

Rest Assured

I sat in a meeting,
And I needed special seating,
Or I would've been caught,
Drifting off in deep thought.

I thought about what was said,
By a guy named Ed.
Thoughts all through my head,
To put things to bed.

People ask what I saw,
And it was a heart I wanted to thaw.
Now I know what I brought,
Simply wasn't sought.

Look inside and you'll find,
A brighter future and clearer mind.
Things aren't always how they seem,
But I still have my self-esteem.
I remember what I bring,
To those who seek a ring.
You can rest assured,
I know how to make a person feel adored.

Once I was knocked off my seat,
But now I stand on my feet.
I used to have a heavy load,
Now I lightly walk down life's road.
The seeds that were sowed,
Will grow in the next episode.

Majestic Potential

I may not look resilient,
But I'm a pillar of strength.
I'm as tiny as a mouse,
And I have to avoid a squirrel's house.

I have sharp edges like a thorn,
But I'm a little acorn.
I have all the tools to succeed,
As long as I'm not used to feed.

When I break out of this suit,
I'll sprout a stalk and a root.
Give me time,
And I will block the sunshine.
This isn't a joke,
I'll become the majestic tree called oak.

Don't judge me in this state,
Judge me at a later date.
You can't see in my heart,
This is only the start.
In time you'll see,
The greatness that resides in me.

A Touch of Glass

This is the game of life so where do I begin?
How many points do I need to win?
The truth is I only need your score,
And when the game is over, I need one point more.

Sometimes the most precious gifts don't cost much,
But somehow manage to deeply touch.
I received another incredible gift as I recall,
It was precious and special kind of ball.

Some of the things that have us feigning,
Are those with a special meaning.
The ball was red and shiny like glass,
A gift for the way I handled things with class.

For as long as I continue living,
That's a gift that'll keep on giving.
It'll remind me of the things I learned,
And inspire me to use the growth I earned.

In a game the ball is used to determine the score,
But in life it tells me to try once more.
So before I go to bed,
I reflect and clear my head.
I look into the ball with sheen like glass,
As a reminder to strive to act with class.

Happy Place

You may wonder why the sudden change.
It may even come across as strange.
One moment I'm filled with hate,
And then suddenly I'm set straight.

What I did looks real cool,
I developed a useful tool.
We usually find what we seek,
This will give you strength when you get weak.

I developed a photo collage,
Of my dreams and me living large.
When there is darkness in my face,
This photo becomes my happy place.

When my train starts getting off track,
I have two ladies to bring it back.
Tiffany on the left, and Eva on the right,
Those two ladies are dynamite.
And no, I don't want two,
But either one of those ladies will do.
When my ghosts start taking me there,
These two ladies bring me back here.

Next is an image of somewhere I'll go one day,
Either for my honeymoon, or for a vacay.
I don't believe for a second that it's out of reach,
One day I'll be on that beach.

I already have my dream car,
But there is another that's on par.
This collage is about striving to succeed,
So dream BIG and not just for what you need.

I know I spend my time like a lawn gnome,
And the last image is of a lovely home.
It's nice and spacious and looks real cool,
And in the back, is a swimming pool.

Build your own collage with whatever you like,
A house, money, spouse, or your dream bike.
And carry a copy to help deal with the things you face,
So you can always escape to your happy place.

Face-to-Face

Being resilient is not a walk in the park,
I found out as I drifted into the dark.
I'm still haunted by painful things,
And I have to recognize danger as soon as the bell rings.

This morning I saw photos of people having fun,
They drank Tequila and danced 'til the night was done.
Suddenly darkness was putting me in a trance,
Painful things abounded, from looking at others dance,
And simply seeing them drink,
Pushed me closer to the brink.

There I was, staring darkness in the face,
As it slowly enveloped my entire place.
Luckily, I had a saving grace,
I changed my perspective, and looked at my happy place.

Looking at the beach, was an incredible sight,
Suddenly my room got really bright.
But to ensure the darkness went away,
I went to my happy place, for an extended stay.
I realize how my day could have been,
And with my happy place, the light will always win

BIG Mistake

Why does it feel like my heart is always breaking?
What is this drastic action I'm thinking of taking?
I can't take this pain anymore,
I'm going to end it, right now, I'm sure.
I give up! I quit!
I take the knife, and slit my wrist.

I'm getting cold; I don't feel too great,
I tried to reverse it, but I've bled out, it's too late.
My spirit stands and looks at my lifeless body on the floor.
My heart broke again, when my wife entered the door.
Even though I'm dead, again I just died,
I watched as my wife broke down and cried.

I thought I had problems before,
I thought my action would end it for sure.
I thought I was hopeless and helpless before,
Now, I'm truly in a position where I can't help anymore.

When I was alive, my pain was my only fact,
But now I'm in a position to see my death's impact.
If I had only taken the time and shared,
Others would have seen my pain and showed that they cared.

As I stand here getting into a dizzy trance,
HE said, "Son, I'll give you another chance."
HE sent me back to the point with the knife,
I immediately dropped it and called my wife.

"Baby I hurt and I don't know what to do,
Please come home, I really need you."
She said, "Honey, I'll be home in just a few,
I've been sick and worried about you."

My wife then refused to leave me alone,
We didn't always talk but she stayed on the phone.
She closed her car door and pressed start.
I said, "Thank you baby, I love you with all of my heart."

A few days later,
When things weren't quite as wild.
I found out what I would've missed,
When my wife said she was with child.

Note: I was inspired to write this while watching a program about re-silience where surviving family and friends spoke about losing a loved one. I agree that suicide is a permanent solution to a temporary prob-lem. Help is available for whatever ails you.

About the Author

 Kollin L. Taylor went through a metamorphosis in his life that resulted in him writing six poetry books from a collection of more than 200 poems written in two months. The pace at which he wrote the poems was why Chaplain Robert A. Miller dubbed him "The Phenom". However, Kollin credits the pace of his writings to his ultimate source of strength and inspiration – **GOD**. He shared some of his life's journey in **Exposed Part I** – *The Prelude*, **Exposed Part II** – *Romantic Relationships*, **Exposed Part III** – *Vida*, **Exposed Part IV** – *...The Journey Continues*, **Metamorphosis** – *The New Me*, and **The Phenom**. The day after submitting *The Phenom* to his publisher, he started working on **Resilience**. He thought he was done spreading the message, but he may have only just begun.

CPSIA information can be obtained at www.ICGtesting.com
Printed in the USA
BVOW041204280213

314287BV00002B/233/P